Contents

THE FINNISH MOSAIC 1
THE HISTORY OF DETERMINATION 2
BLONDE AND BEAUTIFUL? 4
HELSINKI AND ELSEWHERE 8
LAND OF A THOUSAND LAKES 11
NOKIALAND 14
SCIENTIA EST POTENTIA 17
FROM NATION STATE TO CIVIC SOCIETY 18
A NATION FOUNDED ON THE KALEVALA 20
ILLUMINISMO FINNICO 22
THE DRIVING FORCES OF CULTURE 24
FROM RUNNING TRACK TO RACE CIRCUIT 26
RYE BREAD AND FINLANDIA VODKA 28
THE FINNISH MENTALITY 31

© 2007 Liisa Suvikumpu and Otava Publishing Company Ltd.

Translated by Pat Humphreys from the Finnish *Tiesitkö tämän Suomesta?*

Layout: Keski-Suomen Sivu Oy
Cover design: Tiina Palokoski

Front cover illustration: Jarkko Mehtälä/Gorilla Picture Agency
Back cover illustrations: Artek, Jarmo Kananen/LKA, Sputnik Oy, Nokia Oyj, Heikki Tabell/Kuvaario, Kimmo von Lüders/Kuvaario

Printed by Otava Book Printing Ltd.
Keuruu 2007

ISBN-13: 978-951-1-21721-3

< Senate Square and the Cathedral, dating from the start of the 19th century, are some of the best known sights of Finland's capital, Helsinki.

The Finnish mosaic

IMPRESSIONS OF FINLAND depend on whose view you seek. Those who live in the other Nordic countries know that Finland has a population of some 5 million who look and behave in more or less the same way as they do themselves, although they speak a completely different language. Some think first of Nokia mobile telephones, intrepid racing drivers or stunning blondes. First-time visitors to the north from further afield may expect an exotic land of eternal winter, not far from the North Pole and even imagine Finland to be the home of polar bears.

The Finns have always cared greatly about what others think of Finland, but how do they perceive their own country? Surveys of Finnish impressions put countless lakes at the top of the list of Finnish characteristics, alongside the sauna, vast forests, unspoiled nature, a caring society, rye bread, determination and Sibelius. Of course the ultimate truth doesn't come simply by comparing stereotypes but together these different impressions are important pieces of the mosaic called Finland.

The birch tree has strong national symbolic value.

The history of determination

Established in 1646, Fagervik Ironworks and its milieu tell of social history and a developing economy.

THE FINNS HAVE a special word for a characteristic that is very important to them. *Sisu* is somewhere between perseverance and obstinacy and is one of the main building blocks of *Finnishness*. They believe that this state of mind has led to all the good things in their country. Without a determination of spirit and a refusal to compromise, many setbacks of history would have proved fateful for this small, poor nation. Every Finn sees the wisdom of their national author, Aleksis Kivi, when he wrote: "Willpower can take a man through granite."

From pagans to papal subjects

Sisu has been needed for thousands of years. The people who arrived at the end of the Ice Age in the territory that is modern Finland would hardly have overcome the harsh natural conditions without major reserves of willpower. Finland has always been a borderland of sorts and frequently a bone of political contention between its neighbours; determination has helped settle clashes. As early as the thirteenth century, the orthodox Novgorodians in the East and the catholic Danes and Swedes in the west, who had spread widely through the Baltic area, were locked in conflict over the heartlands of Finland.

The heathen Finnish tribes, living off rich fisheries and game, believed in spirits of nature such as Ukko and Ahti, the father god and water god, but they were peaceful people who submitted to Christianity during the Middle Ages without much resistance or bloodshed. Admittedly legend has it that Finnish *sisu* raised its head in the mid-12th century when a peasant named Lalli took exception to catholic Bishop Henrik, who had arrived from Sweden to convert Finns, and struck him dead with an axe. Henrik became the patron saint of Finland and stubborn Lalli the hero of the people.

Over 600 years a part of Sweden

The cultural and commercial linkages of the Baltic region shaped Finland strongly from medieval times onwards as the Finns became active participants in the international Hansa League, which united east and west. With its produce from hunting, gathering and agriculture, Finland joined the networks of the world economy.

The latter Middle Ages were a time of internal progress, when the eastern border became established, castles and stone churches were built, the country's own intelligentsia was educated in foreign universities and conditions were thus fostered for future cultural development. Finland's first written language was Latin, followed by Swedish. With the reformation, the evangelical Lutheran church became established in Finland in the sixteenth century and literature in the national language was created.

Building and drawing borders

The modern era began with wars lasting hundreds of years that made heavy demands on the *sisu* of the Finns. In the Thirty Years' War, Finnish soldiers known as *hakkapeliittas* fearlessly charged the field of battle, urging each other on with dreadful shouts in Finnish.

There was a constant state of war between Sweden and Russia, which was a heavy burden for all of Finland because of military recruitment and high taxes. However the wars of the seventeenth and eighteenth centuries had important incidental consequences; international trade in tar and timber developed to serve shipbuilding, the potato became the main source of nourishment for the people and strong sea fortresses were built in the Gulf of Finland, Sveaborg protecting Helsinki and Svartholma off Loviisa, further to the east.

◁ The Maid of Finland battles Russia's two-headed eagle in Eetu Isto's propagandistic *The Attack* (1899).

A century as a Russian grand duchy

With the concept of spheres of influence in Europe during the Napoleonic Wars and after the Swedish military defeat in 1809, Finland fell under Russian control after more than 600 years as a part of Sweden. The Russians Tsar made Finland into an autonomous grand duchy, a status which was soon being emphasized both culturally and politically in line with the prevailing national romantic mood. Helsinki was developed into the capital city, national organs of government were created and artistic life began to flourish amid a strongly nationalistic spirit, greatly due to the influence of the poet J. L. Runeberg.

Industry and the towns developed rapidly from the start of the nineteenth century onwards; sawmills and related liberalism gave a strong boost to economic development. Nevertheless Finland remained largely agrarian well into the twentieth century; the economy has been dominated by processing of agricultural and forest products up to the present day.

An independent republic since 1917

The political situation was already unstable and, over time, efforts to impose a more Russian character on Finland led to unrest and growing aspirations for independence. The labour movement achieved a breakthrough in the General Strike of 1905 and at the same time the women's and temperance movements became much stronger. Taking advantage of the First World War and the Russian Revolution, Finland declared itself independent in 1917. Internal dissension then led to a bloody civil war in the following spring, deferring the building of a new nation, which was then begun on the terms of the victorious "White" forces.

Although a monarchy was initially envisaged, a president was soon elected and Finland became a parliamentary republic. Living standards rose and services increased apace. Health care, social services and secondary schooling spread to the countryside, too.

From Winter War to Olympics

Finland found itself at war after refusing Stalin's ultimatums. The short Winter War generated much sympathy abroad for a small country fighting doggedly against its large neighbour but, after a large-scale and bloody Soviet assault, Finland was forced to sue for peace. It made large territorial concessions to its aggressor, mostly in Karelia.

During the Interim Peace, Finland made arrangements to assist Germany and, when the Soviet Union bombed Finland again in summer 1941, the Finns joined the war alongside the Germans against a common eastern enemy. Initial success deteriorated into a long period of trench warfare and, in the wake of a large-scale Soviet push, the Finns were forced to concede the enemy's superiority.

Nevertheless, Finland was not occupied and the country remained completely independent as a western democracy, although the onerous peace terms included new territorial losses and economic obligations. Payment of reparations, which gave a strong impetus to the development of an engineering industry, continued until 1952. In the same year – as if to symbolize national determination, peace and rebuilding – the Olympics were held in Helsinki and Armi Kuusela of Finland became Miss Universe.

A model country

After the war Finland set out to build a welfare state, largely on the Swedish model. Modernization in Finland, unlike elsewhere in Europe, ultimately took place very quickly: urbanization, industrialization and the creation of a service economy all at the same time, not consecutively. By the 21st century national *sisu* had made the country into a leader in education, welfare and technology.

Blonde and beautiful?

AT FIRST ACQUAINTANCE, it may seem that all Finns are tall, blond Vikings, that all the men are called *Mika* and that all surnames end with *nen*. In fact the Finns are a mixture of many linguistic and racial features. According to modern studies about three-quarters of the Finnish genotype originates from west and south and a quarter from the east, so among the blond Scandinavian facial shapes there is a dash of eastern features. Plenty of people have dark hair and brown eyes. Finns generally regard themselves as an ethnic mixture.

Origin of the early Finns

The origin of the Finns has always been obscure. Over the centuries countless domestic and foreign researchers have studied where they lived before they settled in the north. The controversial racial theories of the past, used mainly for political propaganda, have disappeared from modern international scientific research. Today it is believed that the forefathers of the Finns arrived on the northern shore of the Gulf of Finland about ten thousand

Many Finns are blond with blue eyes. >

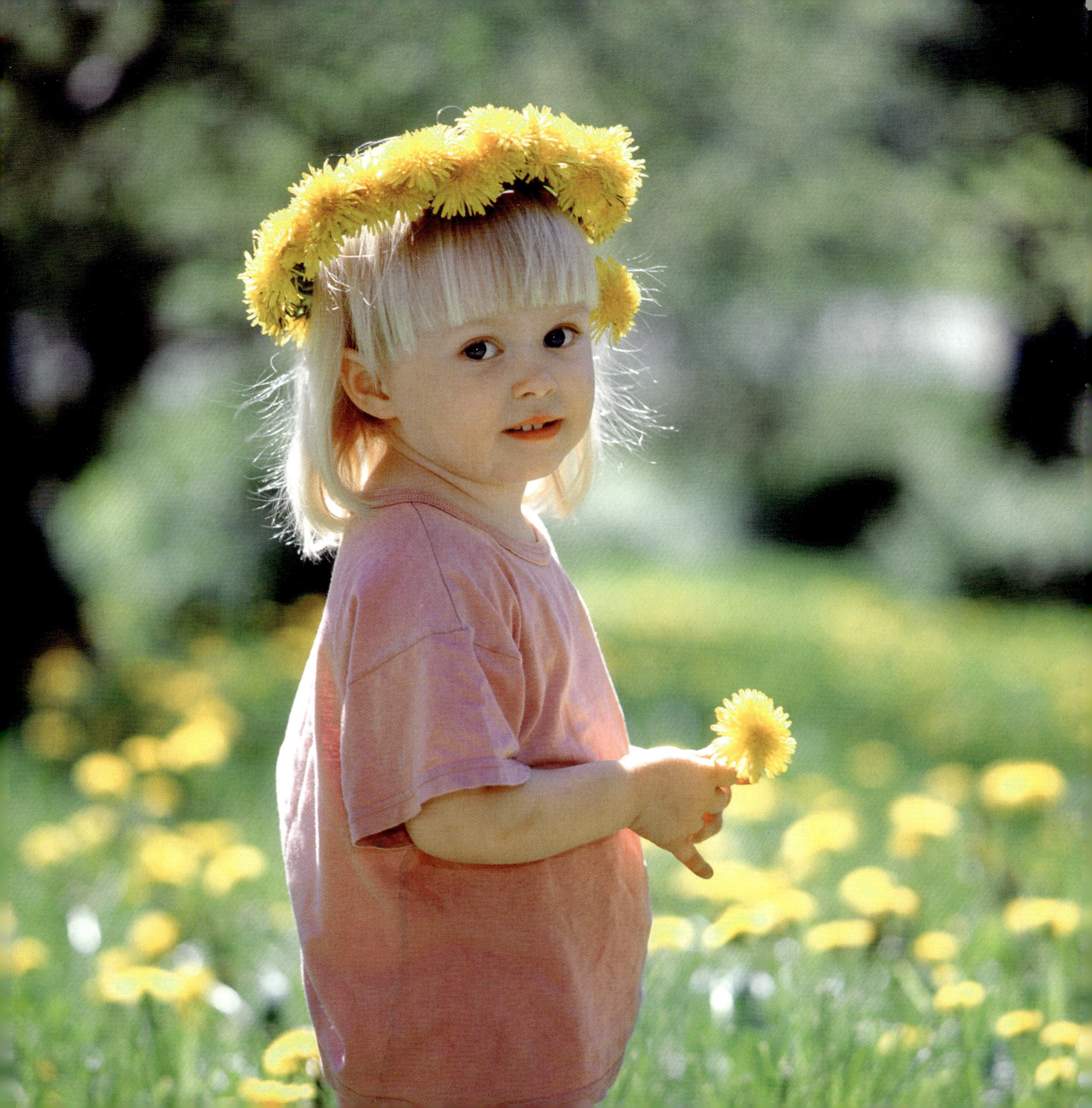

In Lapland reindeer herding is an important livelihood for more than just Santa Claus.

years ago after the Ice Age from areas south and southeast of the Baltic. The Finnish genotype is predominantly Indo-European.

In his book *Germania* in AD 98, the Roman historian Tacitus wrote about a poor but happy race called the Fenni. "Unafraid of anything that man or god can do to them, they have reached a state that few can attain, … so well content that they do not even need to pray for anything," Despite an unfavourable climate and difficult living conditions, these determined ancients put down roots in the hunting and fishing grounds of southern and south western Finland, the areas with the densest population to this day.

Various Finnish cultures

Apparently the *Fenni* were actually the Sami people who subsequently moved ever northward as herders and live today in Lapland, a territory which reaches into Norwegian, Swedish and Russian territory as well as Finland. The Sami are the only indigenous people in the European Union, and they enjoy guarantees of cultural autonomy in Finland today. They have the right to be educated in their own mother tongue and they may use it to conduct official business. The Sami in Finland, numbering about seven thousand, have a very vital culture, with their own artists and even rap musicians.

The historic minorities of Finland are Romas, Russians, Jews and Tatars. Only after the war were measures taken to safeguard minority cultures. There are immigrants from numerous countries in modern Finland, the largest groups being Russians, Estonians, Swedes and Somalis. Despite criticism of it, Finnish policy on refugees remains one of the toughest in Europe.

Official languages Finnish and Swedish

The Finns who speak Swedish as their mother language (about six percent) are an integral part of the population. Until the end of the nineteenth century Swedish was the language of Finnish government and science and was spoken by all educated classes. The Swedish speakers, who today live mainly in southern Finland and along the coast, stoutly maintain their own language as well as their culture although admittedly it differs little from the mainstream culture. They have their own Swedish-speaking institutions, schools, universities, theatres, etc.

Because Finland is a bilingual country, in which Finnish and Swedish have equal status, all Finnish schoolchildren study a "second mother tongue", Finnish speakers Swedish and Swedish speakers Finnish. The Swedish language is strongest in the Åland Islands, the part of Finland where only it has official status. This archipelago, located off the southwest coast and demilitarized by international treaty, has an autonomous government that protects its distinctive culture.

The enigmatic Finnish language

The established relationship between Finnish and other Finno-Ugric languages spoken by small nations like Estonia and Hungary on the European periphery is one clue to the origin of the Finns.

Unfortunately it is far from unambiguous. Finns and Estonians can understand each other to some extent but in practice a Hungarian and a Finn have no idea what the other is saying.

The Finnish language has numerous loan words from other languages, especially from Swedish and German and also from Russian. Furthermore, many Finnish names are derived from common European Christian roots such as Christian = Risto, Birgitta = Pirkko and Mikael = Mika. Most original Finnish names mean something. They may be derived from nature such as Virpi = a slender branch, or from Finnish legends such as Väinö, the hero of the national epic.

Because few others understand what they are trying to express, Finns have always had to learn the languages of others. Today they learn at least two foreign languages at school, many children three or four. They have strong practical language skills and almost everyone understands and speaks English to some extent.

The Finnish woman's strong image

The most conventional image of a Finnish woman is still related to the agrarian period before modern times. A beautiful blue-eyed maiden in national costume, with red cheeks and thick golden-blond plaits, smiles shyly amid a hayfield in front of a red farmhouse. A Finnish woman of the 21st century probably lives in an owner-occupied brick and concrete apartment building in a largish town. She has a university degree and 1.7 children. She is divorced from her first husband and her hobbies are Nordic walking or exercising in the gym. The modern woman lives in a society that regards firm equality and female independence as axiomatic.

< Aki Kaurismäki's unique take on everyday reality in Finland has brought a worldwide reputation for this film director.

Helsinki and elsewhere

MOST OF THE foreigners who travel to Finland arrive in Helsinki at some point. Also a large proportion of Finns have ended up in Helsinki. More than a million people live in the city and the surrounding metropolitan area, where the population density is the greatest in the country. The nation's capital is not merely the centre of government but also the focal point of business life, culture and science. Another advantage is that it is a short distance from many northern European centres, such as St. Petersburg and the Scandinavian and Baltic countries. No wonder Helsinki is one of Europe's most popular congress venues and cruise ports.

Helsinki looks like a fairly typical European capital, with its buildings from different periods, its commercial districts and various residential areas. Situated on the shore of the Baltic Sea and partly on islands, the city is compact, and it is practical to walk anywhere in its centre. Quiet, clean and green are words that describe it well; its air is fresh.

From country to town and back

The exodus from the countryside to the towns that began with economic restructuring in the 1960s has not really ended yet. At the same time, it has been offset by a return of pensioners, who are retiring ever earlier and want to live in the country or in a small town far from the hectic cities. In addition, many families are opting for soft values by moving out of the cities in order to give their children a more peaceful place to grow up. Recent technological developments have also improved the prospects for less dense settlement; telecommuting has become more common and communications networks cover the whole country.

< Nordic walking for peak fitness has become everyman's hobby, on city streets as well as forest paths.

The move back to the country is not, however, sufficient to resettle large abandoned regions in the north, where the population density is sometimes even less than two people per square kilometre. Steps are being taken to ensure services in sparsely populated areas. For example the national government is seeking to decentralize its operations more broadly and many government departments are moving away from the residential and business centres of southern Finland. Many a northern municipality has also found its own niche and developed an image as a core area for a certain service or type of business.

Home ownership and summer cottages

Finland has no slums; quiet dormitory suburbs full of park areas surround almost all its towns. Finnish families favour individual or terraced houses and like to have their own gardens.

Young people leave home at a fairly early age, usually right after upper secondary school. The tendency to early independence is promoted by inexpensive student housing and study grants. Among those of working age, home ownership is more common than in most other countries but, because of high prices, homes are not very spacious. On the other hand, the standard of living and quality of life are boosted by the fact that many Finns also own a second leisure dwelling that is used more or less around the year.

A summer cottage is indeed one of the most typical features of Finnish life. Numbering nearly 470 thousand they ensure an unbroken contact with nature, the countryside and the forest. The folk song *Best Beloved Land* tells of building a cottage "on every cape, in every hollow, for every island" and the urge has not been lost to this day. Despite the mosquitoes, rainy summers, fireplaces that smoke and grills that burn the food, the Finns love cottage life. Common sense might say that it is not worth maintaining a cottage that is used only a few times a year or that senior citizens aren't strong enough for heavy outdoor work, but nothing can extinguish the deep love of a Finn for his own cottage. It is a victory of sentiment over reason.

> Ice hole swimming is popular both in the countryside and at swimming places in towns.

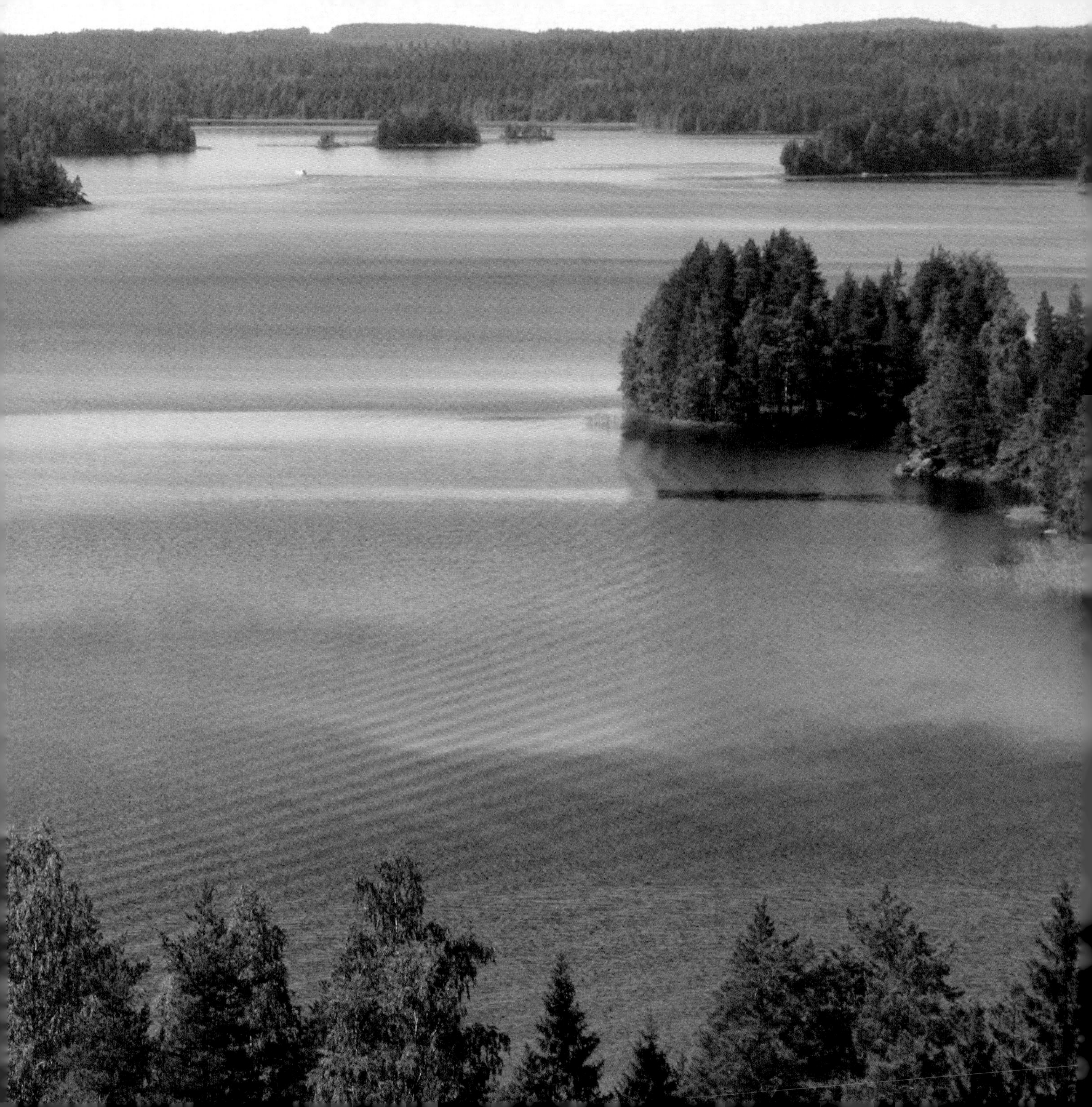

Land of a Thousand Lakes

NOT FOR NOTHING is Finland described as the land of a thousand lakes. It is almost impossible to avoid them, as the visitor soon realises. If he is not taken to the sauna and to a lake to swim, he will be living near one or at least he will see one from the window of his aircraft or car on the way to his destination. The lakes in Finland actually number about 190 thousand, the most in the world. They are simply an inseparable part of the country.

The Finns are so enthusiastic about lakes that, in surveys, they describe the ideal place to live as the centre of a large town in a red cottage on the shore of a lake. A lake brings many advantages, and not merely because it looks beautiful, provides fishing and allows water sports. Its clean clear waters are a strong symbol of the Finnish mindset in favour of peace, calm and security.

Dense forests

Apart from the lakes, rivers, sea inlets and other water features, Finnish nature is dominated by the forests. This should really be described as the land of a thousand forests or a million trees, because woodland covers two-thirds of the country. Great coniferous forests are characteristic throughout the country; the hardwood zone is in the very south and only the far north is above the timber line or where mountain birches grow. Finns think it is obvious that nature should not be polluted and take environmental protection very seriously. In the sustainable development index of the World Economic Forum, Finland has repeatedly been placed first.

Forests have always provided the most livelihoods and been vital for survival. The Finns have progressed from ash farming and tar production to a major forest industry and highly refined products. Apart from their economic significance, however, the forests are also important as a resource for spiritual renewal. The country has no soaring mountains; it is in the vast untouched forests and hills that Finns experience nature and a sense of authenticity.

Nature for activity and tranquillity

The most practical way of enjoying the forest is to hunt and fish; collecting berries and mushrooms are also common pastimes. Wilderness hikes, ski trekking, bird watching and canoeing are very popular forms of exercise in the outdoors, in which the sense of adventure plays an important role. In the vicinity of even the largest towns there are protected forests or national parks suitable for outdoor activities and hiking. The path to a personal retreat in the forest is short and well worn.

Bright summers and cold winters

It comes as a surprise to many foreigners that Finland in summer can be as warm as the Mediterranean. The charts of average temperatures don't show the sweltering days of July, when the towns empty as urbanites head off to their cottages to cool down. In the far north there are fewer hot days but the nightless night continues from May to July. Bright summer nights may make it hard to sleep but the Finns couldn't live without them.

For some people, it may be even more surprising than the summer heat that only ordinary grizzly bears live in Finland, and no polar bears at all. Admittedly more than a third of the country is above the arctic circle and the temperature on the coldest days of winter can drop below -30° C but, like the heat waves of summer, the coldest snaps do not last long. When the snow has formed a firm crust or the water is covered with thick ice,

< The Pisamalahti hill fort in Sulkava offers one of Finland's finest lake panoramas.

sunny winter days can be enjoyed outside on foot, skates, skis or sleds.

Nature sets the pace

There are great seasonal variations and the seasons change at different times in a country that is 1160 kilometres long from north to south. When southerners are already enjoying the first crocuses of spring, the sunniest skiing weather is just starting in the north. The clear definition of the seasons gives Finnish life a distinct rhythm, even in modern towns.

The coldest and darkest period of winter is spent in the security of solidly constructed homes. People work hard and spend their free time visiting each other or in celebrations. Technology can also be used to fight the dark; for example bright light therapy is a popular way of getting more energy and a good mood. Primeval forces, in turn are represented by the northern lights; the *aurora borealis* lights up the winter night sky mainly in northern Finland but sometimes even in Helsinki.

People like to spend as much as possible of their holiday during the summer, when they can enjoy it outdoors. From midsummer onwards, most Finns spend a month on vacation at their cottages, on sailing boats or travelling. For schoolchildren summer is the best of times; the school recess is more than two months long.

The Finns are very connected to nature and have a high appreciation of the value of unspoiled living conditions in their native country.

< The Northern Lights can best be seen in Lapland's winter night skies.

The appeal of nature is irresistible on > bright summer nights.

FIND OUT ABOUT FINLAND

Nokialand

FOR CENTURIES THIS small country with its low population spent a quiet existence on the fringes of northern Europe, living mainly from agriculture and its forests. Suddenly, at the turn of the 21st century, a small miracle and a large amount of effort transformed it into a pioneer and model for technological development. With the success of its mobile phone producer, Finland became known to the world as Nokialand.

Finnish industry and business have been vigorous restructured over a few decades. The transition from centralized economic planning to free market economics has taken place via a revolutionary shake-up of its business sectors.

From forest products to telecommunications

Finnish economic history differs from that of traditional industrial countries. Its industrialization began late but the transition from capital, labour and material-intensive manufacturing to knowledge-based production was rapid. Total output increased strongly after the war and by the 1980s various sectors of industry began to develop in the direction of high technology faster than in other European countries.

After a slump at the start of the 1990s, productivity grew at one of the fastest rates in the world. New sectors developed alongside traditional branches of industry. Forest products and engineering were dethroned by electronics and high technology. Today international surveys rate Finland as one of the world's most competitive and innovative countries.

Top of many classes

Agriculture, previously the main livelihood, has steadily lost importance in the national economy but domestic food production is still very important to the Finns. Bio-dynamic food, locally produced from pure local ingredients, still outflanks the competition on the market square and hypermarket counter. Farmed Finnish strawberries are the world's best berries – if you ask a Finn.

Papermaking and pulping continue to be important businesses and Finland is one of the world's leading producers in this sector. Today, though, you will also encounter Finland in many other connections around the world, whether using Kone lifts, lazing on a luxury cruise ship in the Caribbean, sailing in a Swan yacht, taking bearings from a Suunto wristop computer, turning an Oras tap, casting a Rapala lure, getting dressed up in

< More and more people are using new technology for telecommuting.

Marimekko or speaking on a Nokia mobile telephone.

In many cases the Finnish product is chosen for its assurance of quality, reliability and individuality.

Future challenges

Finland's dependency on Nokia has been criticized as excessive, sometimes strongly so. Economists warn of the dangers of a one-horse economy and humanists are worried about losing the traditional Finnish set of values as a few people become suddenly rich.

On the other hand many countries dream of having their own Nokias and visitors come from abroad to study ethical business practices. In any case the linkage between Nokia and the national image and culture is a reality and it is impossible to understand 21st century Finland without it.

Amid accelerating globalization and competition in the world economy, it will be a tough challenge for a small country to keep up, and Nokia alone will not determine Finland's future. IT expertise, biotechnology and the learning sector are regarded as keys to future economic dynamism. Making the business environment more conducive to innovation is indeed the main national project for the years ahead.

Finns have a wide range of skills. They design icebreakers as well as mobile phones.

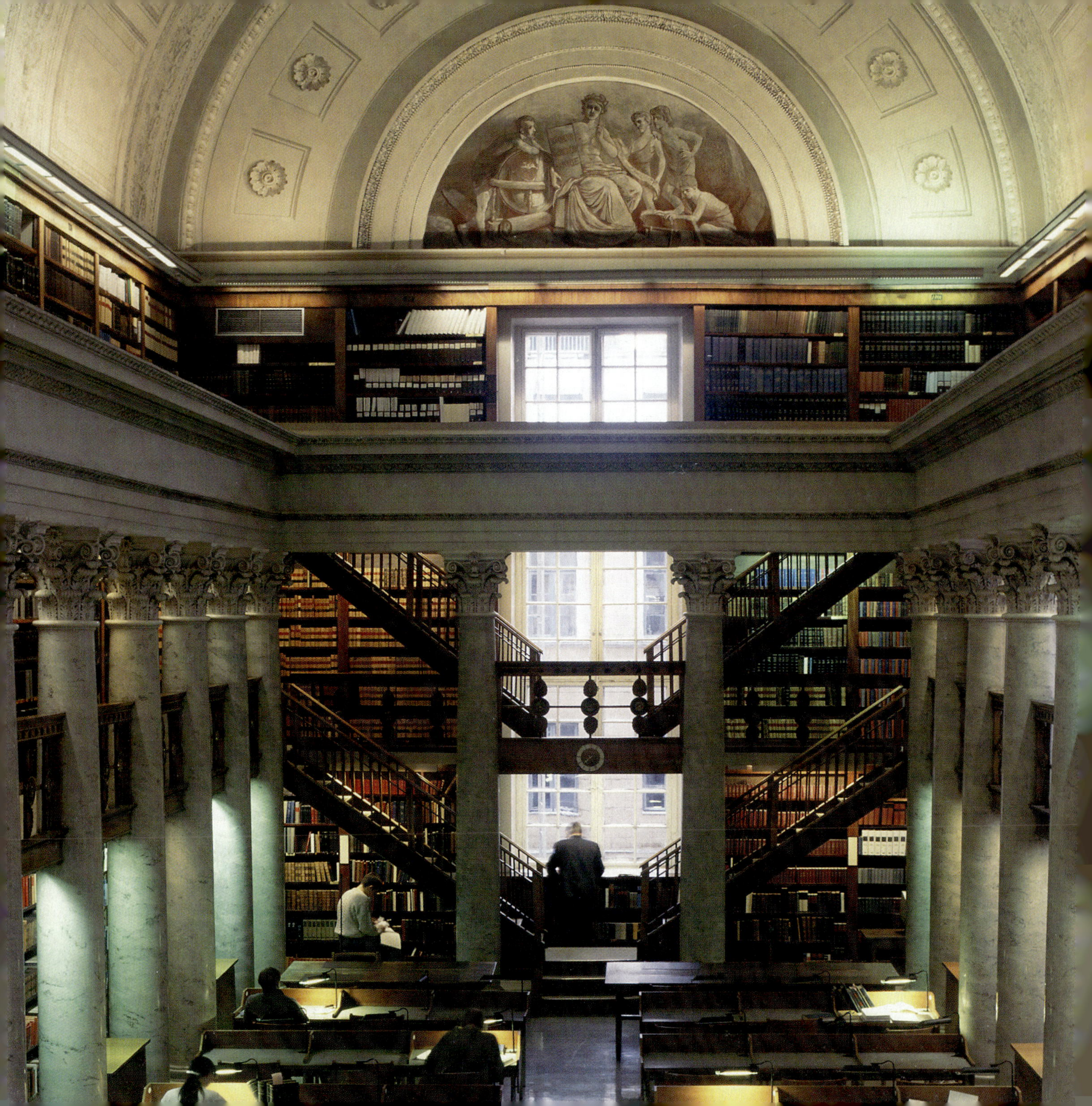

FIND OUT ABOUT FINLAND

"Scientia est potentia"

LIFELONG LEARNING IS a phrase often heard in Finland, and it is also believed. The emphasis is on learning from cradle to grave and investment in education is encouraged at both the individual and the corporate level. People believe that the welfare state and the knowledge-based society should be developed in tandem, and that the latest achievements of science should be applied quickly and effectively in all fields of life.

Over the past few years, extra efforts have been made to disseminate information about science, at the same time as traditional forms of education have evolved. Adult institute courses, public university lectures and the libraries are full of people who genuinely thirst for knowledge and culture and are spontaneously trying to improve themselves. Adult education has become an ever more important part of national education planning and policy.

< Helsinki University library is a paradise for researchers and friends of architecture.

Finnish children have repeatedly topped the league in various areas of the OECD's Programme for International Student Assessment (PISA). >

A society that values education

Schooling has always been highly esteemed, as have educational quality and equal opportunity. A reform in the school system in the 1970s meant that all Finnish children were accorded equal rights and obligations to study for nine years without charge. Teaching, teaching material and school dinners are financed by the government for all between the ages of seven and sixteen. After basic schooling the majority of young people continue in either an upper secondary school or a vocational school: two-thirds of Finns have some kind of higher education qualification.

Although children begin school relatively late compared with many other countries, the first school is often preceded by many years of kindergarten and a year in pre-school. In kindergartens, organized by local municipalities, children practice reading and arithmetic but above all they learn group work skills and self expression via playing. Music colleges and other government-supported cultural facilities provide additional high-quality education for children in their free time from an early age.

The value of human capital

There is a dense network of university-level institutes that practically covers the whole country. Teaching is financed mainly from tax revenues and students receive a monthly study grant. The majority of university students are women. An ever increasing proportion of them spent a year as exchange students abroad. Correspondingly an ever larger number of foreign students come to Finland.

A special strength of the education system is close cooperation between business and universities. Vocational institutes and universities have good resources for high quality teaching, and

Tor Wennström Lehtikuva

the laboratories, computers, software, libraries, etc. at the disposal of students are excellent by international standards. A special feature is the emphasis on teaching and using Latin, and Finland's weekly Latin news bulletin *Nuntii latinii* has listeners all around the world.

Research is financed from both public and private funds. Apart from the central government, private foundations are important donors to science and the arts and can support innovative projects of greater risk than public sources can. Great attention is paid to technological innovation and renewal in education and scientific curricula. At the same time, basic studies in the humanities, though "economically unproductive", are highly esteemed as an obvious cornerstone of civilization. In research, hard and soft values are in balance.

From nation state to civic society

FINLAND'S CONSTITUTIONAL CONTINUITY has spanned a relatively long period of time, and strong social and economic change. Political conflicts during the period of autonomy and in the early years of independence gave rise to a disparate multiparty system that was prone to disputes, but it has proved to be extremely stable. The party political field is characterised by approval of the status quo in all major issues of substance. Finland has seen little political radicalism compared with many other European countries. Its society is a rather homogenous culture of consensus.

The pyramid of parliament, government and president

The first organs of national government were created in 1809 at the time when was Finland was separated from Sweden to become an autonomous grand duchy of Russia. In the words of Tsar Alexander I, it was now "a nation among the family of nations". The Governing Council established at that time was later to become the Imperial Finnish Senate. After independence, its name was changed to the Council of State, and its administrative departments became ministries.

Sovereign power in Finland belongs to the people, represented by parliament convened in parliamentary session. The parliament is unicameral and consists of 200 members. Those over the age of 18 have the right to vote and to stand for election. The parliamentary term lasts four years. There has generally been a non-socialist majority in parliament but the party enjoying the greatest support has long been the Social Democratic Party (SDP). Female politicians have long been active in running Finland, which in 1906 became the first European country to give women the vote and equal political rights Today about 35-40% of the members of parliament are women. The first female president of the republic, Tarja Halonen, was elected in 2000.

The powers of the president have been reduced but he or she has a senior role,

Everyday politics are eagerly debated > over coffee and cakes at market square throughout the country.

LA FINLANDIA DA SCOPRIRE

in cooperation with the government, in determining foreign and security policies. The presidential term lasts six years and the maximum number of terms that can be served is two. The government is formed by a prime minister, chosen by parliament, generally the leader of the party that received the greatest number of votes in the election. The number of ministers can vary; generally there are 15-20, about half of them women. The effectiveness of Finland's administration has been recognised within the EU.

A nation founded on the Kalevala

THE SPIRITS OF forest and water, the struggle between good and evil, brave heroes and fabulous riches are the main themes of Finland's national epic, the Kalevala. With singing and rhyming the ancient Finnish people created the basis for a unique tapestry of stories that was written down at the start of the nineteenth century. These tales have in turn inspired Finns again and again in the fields of pictorial art, music and literature. The mythical, primordial songs and incantations of the Kalevala are a living part of Finnish culture to this day.

The history of literature written in Finnish goes back no farther than the 16th century but it is preceded by a strong oral tradition rooted in the obscurity of prehistory. These ancient runes were the strongest stimulus for the outburst of national romanticism. The unique tradition of story telling was seen as a mark of the Finnish nation state's legitimacy and a primeval cultural kinship,

> The Finnish Moomintroll family is loved throughout the world.

The Defence of the Sampo (1896) by Akseli Gallen-Kallela brings a powerful dynamic to illustration of the national epic, *The Kalevala*.

a sequel to the epic tradition of ancient Greece. The tales of the Kalevala also catalyzed Finnish national art and the description of common people in the 19th century, when Finnish literature actually began to flourish.

The Finnish vantage point

The position of literature as a building block of Finnish identity is undisputed. Reading has always been esteemed, as have writers, who easily achieve celebrity status even today. This may partly be due to the long storytelling tradition, in which the treasured "wisdom of the elders" was relayed to new generations.

Narrative methods have changed but even modern artists often portray *Finnishness*. Although other themes have naturally risen to equal stature, the interpretation of being Finnish is the origin and climax of many a modern work. Aki Kaurismäki's cinematographic storytelling, Arto Paasilinna's humoristic novels or Eija-Liisa Ahtila's video installations can be understood as treatments of universal subjects but the stories at their core are specifically a description of being Finnish and seeing the world from a Finnish viewpoint.

The most individual and best-loved Finnish story telling is contained in the world of the Moomins and their adventures. The characters created by Tove Jansson are widely known around the world and adults, too, have enjoyed these philosophical children's stories. The Moomins reflect the way Finnish people see the world. Northern melancholy and mythic secrecy are communicated in their closeness to nature, their wintry atmosphere, their monster stories and their harrowing loneliness. But self irony and delight in tiny things are other symptoms of the Moomins and the Finnish mentality.

Illuminismo finnico

THE POIGNANCY OF Finnish art is in the beauty of simplicity, which approaches the austere. Stone Age peoples drew minimalist symbols of nature on cliffs, medieval church builders gave granite blocks a divine sensitivity, national romantics captured the Finnish soul in art and music, modern rationalists breathe life into glass and wooden objects. Wisdom in Finland is never complex.

This active world of art has been made possible in part by the successful grant policies of the government and private donors. Public support for culture is part of Finnish welfare and basic services.

Dynamic pictorial art

The golden age of national painting was the *fin de siècle*, when European influences forced their way into Finnish studios. Works of impressionism, realism and symbolism are still some of Finland's most valued pictures. A few of the artists of the golden age became true national heroes, whose imagery, especially in portraying the life of the people, has shaped the Finnish identity very strongly. In the past few decades the appreciation of women artists has risen apace. A concrete example is Helene Schjerfbeck, whose pictures at auction have obtained some of the highest prices paid for Finnish art.

Interest in visual art is strong. There are various extremely popular courses; many trained and self-taught artists; and galleries and exhibitions of a high standard around the country. Photography in particular has risen rapidly in esteem, even as a form of home decoration. Video installations in turn have found a strong following at exhibitions.

< Alvar Aalto's line is famous both in architecture and design. Savoy vase (1937).

Starting from beauty and function

In Finnish design at its most typical, clarity of shape and usefulness of purpose form a harmonious union. It could be said that the reason for the success of products by Nokia, Suunto and others is not merely their technical prowess but their supreme sense of style and function. Finnish designers have had a central role in creating the Swedish-Danish-Finnish style that is known as Scandinavian design.

The triumphal march of Finnish design that began in the 1950s is largely based on the innovative views of a few master designers. Skilled artisans have understood how to give design a tangible form and have grasped the opportunities offered by materials. Modern Finnish designers have attained their great reach and stature from a position on the shoulders of these giants. Meanwhile, young designers are breaking through traditional boundaries and adopting entirely new approaches.

The ideal of simplicity

Finland's architects follow largely the same ideals as its designers. Simplicity, clarity, purpose and individuality are their guiding lights and make them easily recognizable. The functionalist language of Alvar Aalto, in particular, has symbolized these inherent characteristics. Finnish architecture, older or more

FIND OUT ABOUT FINLAND

modern, also radiates a unique northern spirit. Indeed, a genuine relationship with nature has been regarded as an important factor when analyzing why Finland is a leading country in the world of architecture.

The building material that is most natural and traditional for the Finns has always been wood and its use today is experiencing a renaissance. Water is another important element. It has become popular to use flowing or dripping water in modern ecclesiastical architecture, even in interiors. Finnish architecture has returned to its springhead and spirituality. It embodies sustainable values, a sense of location and an expression of permanence.

< In the Forest Hall of Lahti's Sibelius Hall (2000), innovative wood architecture unites the building traditions of Finland, old and new.

The driving forces of culture

WHAT DOES THE New York Metropolitan Opera have in common with heavy metal festivals, the tango or a stringed instrument called the kantele? The unifying factor is Finland's passion for music. For some people, the essence of being Finnish is the sound of an accordion carrying from the opposite shore on the nightless night of Midsummer. For others it is *Valse Triste* by Jean Sibelius, played at the Finlandia Hall under the baton of Esa-Pekka Salonen. At its most basic it is a Kantele player in national costume, rendering a melancholy folk tune. In all its different forms music has an unshakeable position in Finland.

Triumph of the classical

There is no single reason for Finland's great status in classical music. The fairly short history of transcribed Finnish music does not explain its present success. But the choral tradition, the progressive and broadly based programme of music education begun in the 19th century and an effective system of grants start to explain the roots of this success story.

Finland's acclaimed opera singers and its conductors who direct some of the finest orchestras around the world are the best-known music makers of Finland but its composers have been in demand, too. Of the most popular composers whose works are performed abroad, Sibelius is still the top name but more recent musicians have also reached prominence, particularly Einojuhani Rautavaara, Magnus Lindberg and Kaija Saariaho.

Heavy metal and tango!

For decades Finns laboured under a serious national inadequacy, their repeated failure in the Eurovision Song Contest. Envy of neighboring Sweden and Estonia came to an end in Athens in spring 2006. The Finnish monster hard rock band Lordi won the contest by a large margin and put its home town of Rovaniemi on the world musical map. In recent years, other light Finnish music as well as rock has risen in popularity around the world as Finland's music business has "grown up".

< The brightest stars in Finland's musical firmament, Karita Mattila in the title role of *Salome* at the Metropolitan Opera...

FIND OUT ABOUT FINLAND

Finland has international talent in all genres although the most successful artists are in metal music. The only successful group outside Europe used to be Hanoi Rocks; today the greatest popularity is enjoyed by HIM and The Rasmus. It's interesting that many of the success stories of Finnish light music have been strongly influenced by the classical, such as the symphonic metal Nightwish and the cello metal Apocalyptica. Even an electronic kantele has been used to play heavy metal.

Domestic hit songs and the tango are intensely alive in Finland. Dance floors and karaoke bars around the country echo nostalgically to evergreen singles, many of which date back to the 1940s and 1950s. The appointment of a Tango King and Tango Queen at each year's Seinäjoki Tango Festival is a similar tradition. And at any party, playing a "Finnhit", a cover version by a Finnish

...and Ville Valo of HIM in a sea of snowballs. >

Michael Johansson   Lehtikuva

artist, will gets almost everyone onto the dance floor or at least tapping their feet enthusiastically to the rhythm.

Dance as a future art form

More and more Finns are becoming interested in dance as an art form. In part this is due to the influence of distinctive, internationally oriented modern dance talents such as Jorma Uotinen and Tero Saarinen and company. Finnish dance has a reputation for high quality and individuality and has received constant critical acclaim in international forums. Finland is putting its efforts behind modern dance and its export, because it is seen as an art form that is independent of language and therefore will speak to people of all countries and cultures.

From running track to race circuit

FINNS ARE SAID to do well in any competition that requires a helmet, such as ski jumping, motorsport or ice hockey. Apparently the balanced Finnish combination of recklessness and imperturbability come together to create the stubbornness that wins helmet events.

Sports clubs have deserved the greatest credit for physical education, in the same way as the schooling systems of other countries, from basic schools to universities, lay the foundations for competitive sports and exercise. The system worked extremely well until the 1950s, when tougher international competition and greater politicization began to push Finland down the points table. Finnish sport without the pressures of professionalism enjoyed its glory days in the inter-war period, when Finnish long-distance runners, in particular, always came first.

Moving sports

The main events that have brought tears to Finnish eyes have been their win in the 1995 ice hockey world championships, the victories of Keke Rosberg, Mika Häkkinen and Kimi Räikkönen in Formula 1 racing and the shameful ski doping scandals. There is continuous public debate about how sports should be financed and why Finns don't do well in prominent competitions, or at least not as well as neighbouring countries.

Sport is important for bolstering the national ego. Regardless of the success of Finnish competitors in international events, their performances are followed closely from Finnish living rooms with unabashed cheers. Ecstatic spectating is a serious national sport.

Snowboarding has quickly become > the craze of competing professionals and amateurs alike.

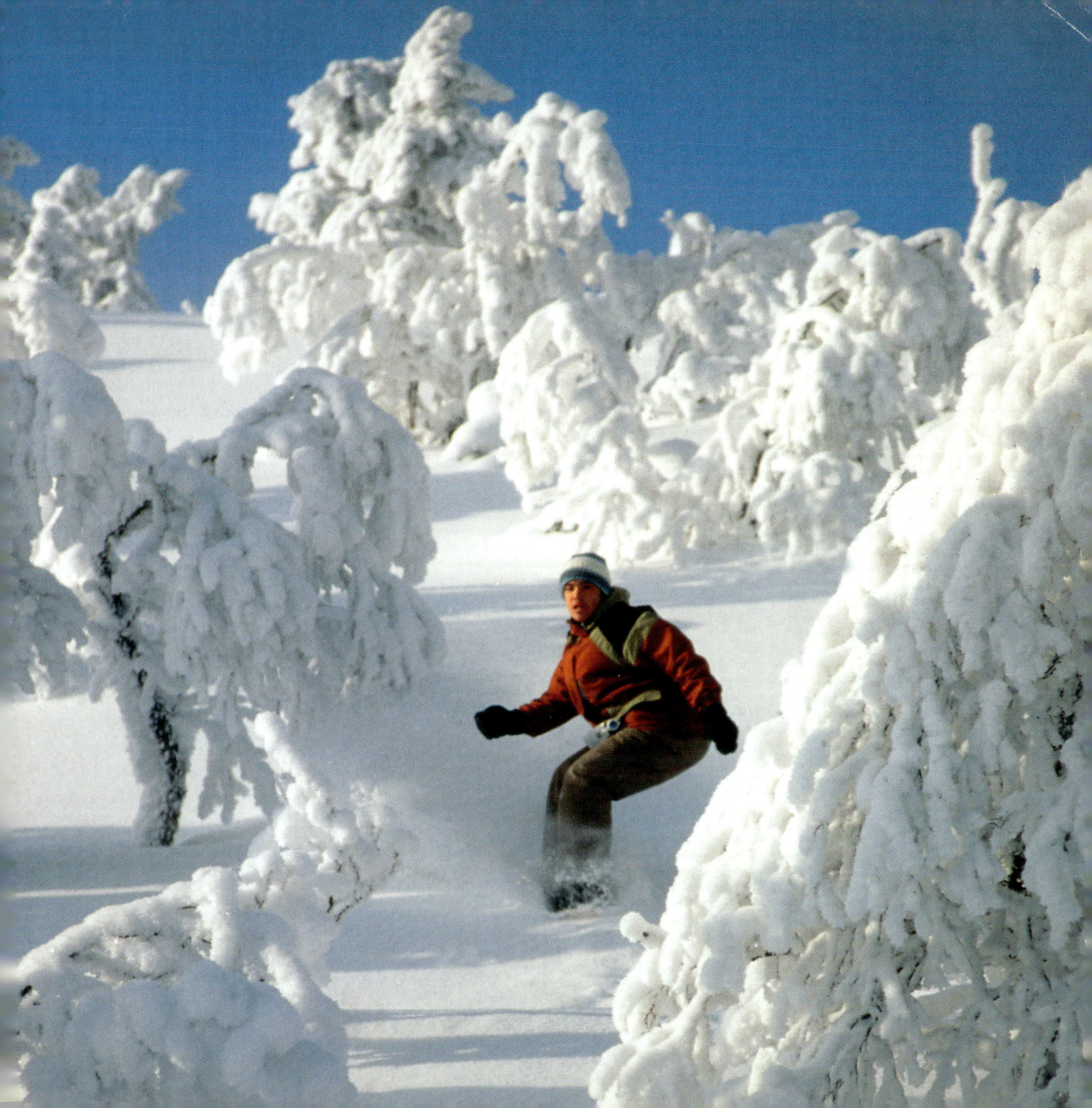

Rye bread and Finlandia vodka

IN MATTERS OF food Finns apply largely the same philosophy as in design, architecture and their general outlook: simple is beautiful. A history of scarcity lasting many centuries has moulded Finnish traditional cuisine and tastes to be basically minimalist. Wealth and the changing structure of livelihoods have expanded Finnish eating habits and epicurean pleasures but national specialities remain a valued part of the banqueting table. Everyday food, however, hardly differs from the European average and international influences show very strongly in the types of restaurants available and the eating habits of the young.

Cuisine has absorbed many influences from Sweden and Russia. The most varied gastronomic innovations have arrived from both east and west in the course of history, from the potato to coffee. The preparation of continental delicacies was learned in early times from high society in Stockholm and Saint Petersburg, and the best cookbooks in Finland have been French for several centuries. Of Scandinavian customs, the most popular is probably the crayfish party, where the consumption of red-shelled cooked crayfish is accompanied by songs to keep up the pace of snaps drinking. Blinis are a special delicacy from the east: fried buckwheat pancakes eaten with fish roe and smetana, plus sips of vodka to refresh the palate. Heavy use of alcohol has always been part of Finnish culture and binge drinking can be brutally obvious in the late evening street scene.

There are plenty of regional specialities left, although eating habits have become more uniform throughout the country. Various gruels, curd cheeses and stuffed pasties were ordinary fare for the common man when each household produced its own food. Salted or smoked fish and game complemented the diet around the year. On the other hand fresh vegetables were not previously available during winter, and the accompaniments to meals were root crops and casseroles prepared from them. In modern times, the most popular form of high-fibre food is undoubtedly rye bread. In all surveys Finns rank it first for its authenticity, its tastiness and also its health-giving properties.

Functional food

After the war, the range of Finnish foods was deliberately expanded in a more healthy direction in a top-down project to change eating habits. In the famous North Karelia project of the 1970s, the people of eastern Finland, who had shunned vegetables in favour of fat, cream and butter, were taught to eat more healthily and live longer by adopting a more Mediterranean cuisine. The food provided from public funds in Finnish schools has been acclaimed around the world; its influence on national health is indisputable.

Measures to promote healthier eating are not just a whim of fashion. This small people with its homogenous gene pool suffers from various sicknesses that are classed as endemic. Cardiovascular disease, diabetes and the spread of numerous allergies can however be controlled fairly well by diet. Gluten and lactose intolerance are especially typical for the Finns, and party fare now automatically includes countless alternatives for people with food sensitivities.

◁ Rye bread has been a firm part of the Finnish diet for centuries.

The interest in improving health and welfare shows in the many patents of the food processing sector and the increased range of products stocked by shops, such as foods containing xylitol. Cholesterol-reducing fats and lactic acid bacteria that bring balance to the digestive tract are just a small part of the range of functional foods that have boosted national welfare in recent years. Non-material values are also being pursued in food production. Local food, biodynamic produce and respect for animal rights show in the choices of informed families as well as in the menus of restaurants, work canteens and school kitchens.

Gourmet delicacies change with the seasons; at the end of summer, crayfish parties are cheery social events.

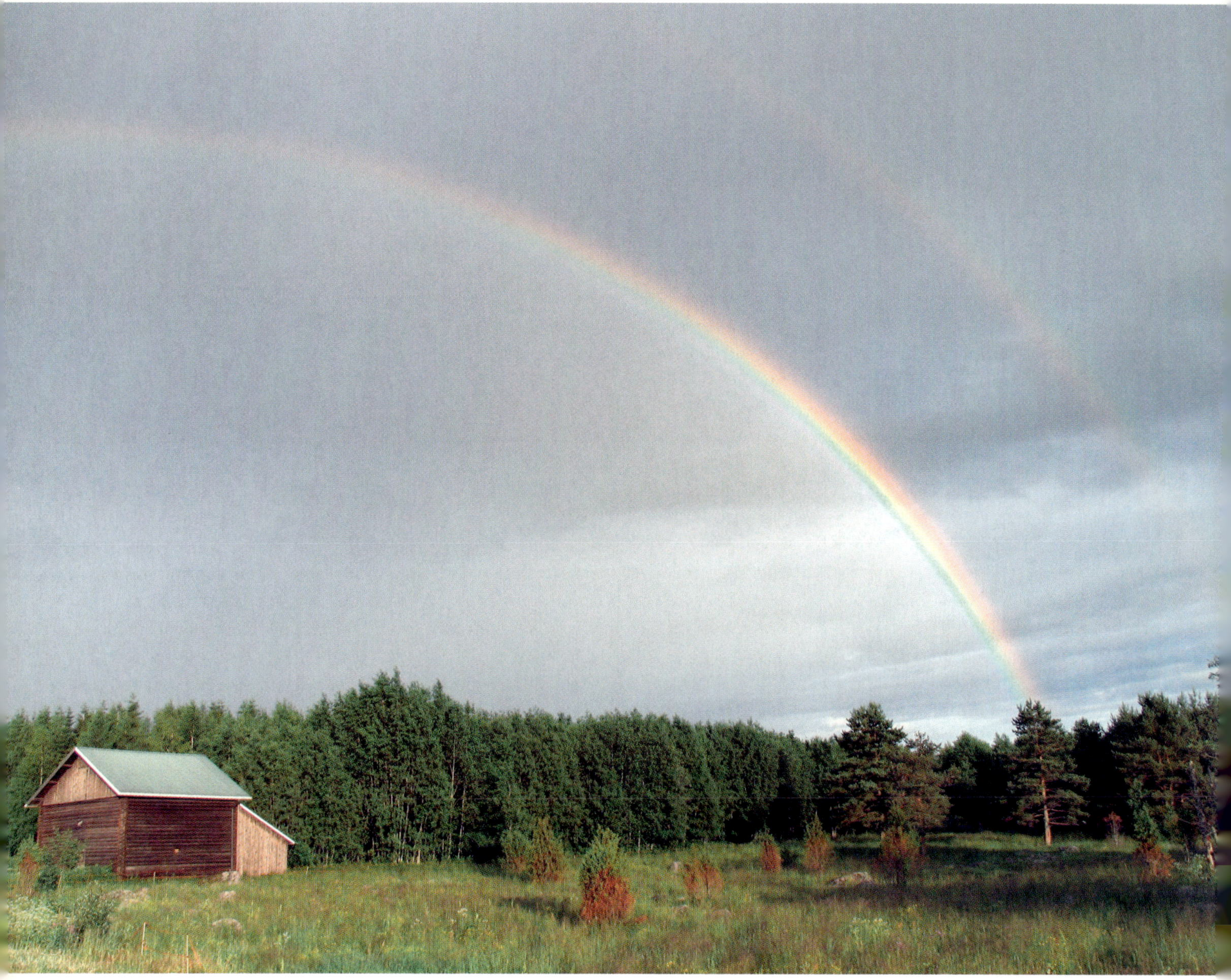

The Finnish mentality

NEWLY INDEPENDENT FINLAND at the start of the 20th century swore by the values of "family, faith and fatherland". In a country traumatized by major wars, the phrase became a summary of the things Finns respect the most. The world has changed, and Finland with it, but the three tenets continue to express core national values.

During the arctic winter, a Finn wants to withdraw to the safety and warmth of his own home. Built with love, the home is an important, almost sacred place to which only close relatives or highly esteemed people are invited. Families don't generally move often and have strong emotional ties with their homes. The home is often synonymous for the family, "at our home" meaning "in our family", where outsiders hold no sway. Some languages don't even have separate words for house and home; in Finnish *home* contains an enormous emotional charge.

Religion is a very personal matter and whether or not someone belongs to the church does not in practice show at all in everyday life. Evangelical Lutherans make up 81% of the population, while 1% belong to the Orthodox Church of Finland. Thirteen percent are members of no religious denomination. Studies show that church and parish matter steadily less to the Finns, particularly for young urbanites, who opt out of formal religion ever more readily. Religious holidays are spent in a rather secular fashion and churchgoing is declining continuously.

Flying the national flag is important; official flag-raising days are marked on the calendar, and the blue cross is hoisted on the flagpole of every house. Flag-raising is used to show respect as much to national poets and authors as to the United Nations, election days and even Midsummer. Although spectators may paint a blue cross on their faces and wave tiny banners, the relationship with the official Finnish flag – and the fatherland – is one of great respect. The celebration of Independence Day on 6th December is always serious and restrained. The candles lit at every window symbolize an ardent silence in honour of the day. A boisterous carnival mood would be unsuitable for expressing the deference that Finns feel towards the independence that cost so much, their fatherland and their own hallowed flag.

< Agrarian nostalgia has a firm hold on modern Finns.

A safe and peaceful country

Foreigners living in Finland will tell that some of its greatest assets are the peace and safety of the environment and the efficiency and integrity of its society. Surveys show that Finns are regarded as honest, trustworthy and friendly. Democracy is strongly entrenched and there is genuine debate on all levels, both privately and in public life. People are encouraged to better themselves and organizations are committed to good governance.

Perhaps one way in which the Finns differ from many other peoples is their admiration for simplicity. They appreciate the basic things of life and don't believe in making a big issue about everything. Some say that the main reason is that high taxes have made materialism impossible. Some of the most negative aspects of Finland are seen as the climate and the taciturn people, although many others regard these characteristics as refreshing. The Finns themselves say that there's no such thing as bad weather, only bad clothing.

Sauna is the key

One of the most mystical parts of the Finnish mosaic is the sauna. This remarkable invention defines Finnishness; sauna is the key to understanding the national mentality. There are countless words and products beginning with sauna, from sauna sausages to sauna gnomes, that tell how central it is to Finnish culture. Although you can find modern saunas everywhere from apartment buildings to exercise gyms, everyone's "best sauna" is bound to be at the family's own summer cottage.

Tucked away on the shore of a quiet lake, hidden from the neighbours' gaze, is a simple wooden shack. On a summer evening, a wisp of white smoke rises from its chimney. Inside the tiny sauna room, birch logs crackle in the stove. Figures swathed in towels hurry down the path to the sauna through the cool air. Soon can be heard the hiss of water on hot stones and the cheery swish of sauna whisks as the bathers beat each other on the back, releasing an intoxicatingly fresh birch smell from the twigs. The naked bathers plop into the clear water at the end of the jetty and swim a few peaceful strokes. Afterwards they sit drowsily and relaxed in front of the sauna enjoying the beauty and calm of nature, their own good moods and perhaps a foaming beer.

The most important decisions and closest friendships in Finland are formed in the sauna. It is a place to go with friends and it is the highest compliment to be invited to spend time at another's sauna. Few words may be exchanged but they will be all the weightier. Hot steam, beautiful surroundings, peace, quiet and primitive conditions; the different elements of sauna combine to create a unique peace of mind which is impossible to describe. It must be experienced.

< Sauna is the key to understanding the Finnish mindset.